T0198986

PERFECTLY

IMPERFECT

Poetry by Nadeera K Vasu

To order additional copies of this book, contact
Toll Free +65 3165 7531 (Singapore)
Toll Free +60 3 3099 4412 (Malaysia)
www.partridgepublishing.com/singapore
orders.singapore@partridgepublishing.com

Because of the dynamic nature of the Internet, any web addresses or links contained in this book may have changed since publication and may no longer be valid. The views expressed in this work are solely those of the author and do not necessarily reflect the views of the publisher, and the publisher hereby disclaims any responsibility for them.

ISBN

978-1-5437-6030-9 (sc)
978-1-5437-6031-6 (e)

Print information available on the last page.

08/28/2020

PARTRIDGE

ABOUT THE AUTHOR

Nadeera K Vasu is a Malaysian-born Writer, Poet, Fashion Model & Youth Activist who often speaks about her personal journey and educates the public on topics related to disability. Being the Very 1st Differently-Abled Model **in Malaysian History**, to go on the runway for "Malaysia Fashion Week 2018", she hopes to do more for the differently-abled community who are often marginalized or forgotten. Being a BSc (Hons) Psychology graduate in The University of Nottingham, she is also passionate about helping others struggling with various mental illnesses and advocating on the importance of mental health in today's society. Nadeera also often expresses her feelings through her writing and poetry. This concise, yet meaningful compilation, will give you a glimpse into the heart & soul of Nadeera.

On 16th April 1992

A Girl Was Born

Weighing only 2.4kgs

Her Body Ever So Brittle

But Her Mind So Strong

"Let Her Go" they said

But Here She Is

At Twenty-Eight

Telling Her Story

In The Form of Poetry

Mother

Mother
You are like no other
Forever ready to smother
Even when your child is such a bother

Mother
When your child does some blunder
You never ever stop to ponder
Neither question nor wonder
'Why do I have such a daughter?'

Mother
Your love, patience & endurance exceeds beyond that of an ordinary other
Just when we think your sacrifices cannot go any farther
You prove us wrong by going one step further

Mother
May you always be that flame of fire
Whom your children choose to aspire
May you have all that you desire
Even though you feel you are about to retire

Father

Father

You are
A daughter's first love
A son's first hero
The very anchor of the family

You are
The shining star in the sky above
Giving me that constant glow
Helping me attain my greatest fantasy

You are
As gentle as a dove
Always there helping me grow
Preventing me from reaching insanity

You are
My night and shining amour
My very own G.I. Joe
Today, tomorrow, and for all eternity

Silence

Silence Oh Silence
What art thou?
Art thou the language of the soul
Or a pole?
Art thou meant for the meek
Or the weak?
Art thou meant to teach
Or to breach?

Silence Oh Silence!
What does thou bringeth?
Immense love?
Overwhelming grief?
Great depth?
Enormous rage?
Spiritual realization?
Embittered friendship?

Silence Oh Silence
What art thou?
What art thou?
What art thou?

When I Look At You

When I look at you

I see beauty
I see perfection
I see plenty
Of tender affection

When I look at you

I see love
I see clarity
I see a dove
With utmost purity

When I look at you

I see resilience
I see deliverance
I see patience
And a soulful benevolence

When I look at you

I feel I stand no chance
For the one in your heart
Seems to consume your every part
But oh my darling, no matter what your stance
Don't you tear our connection apart

One Wrong Move

One Wrong Move
And the whole world comes crumbling down

One Wrong Move
And you're always gonna be looked upon with a frown

One Wrong Move
Everything you are forced to forget
And you're left to face a lifetime of regret

One Wrong Move
And all your good is washed away
And only the bad is here to stay

One Wrong Move
And you seem to disapprove
Even the slightest groove

But hey,
One Wrong Move
Does not mean I am not trying to improve

One Wrong Move
Does not make me foolish
Or ruthless and selfish
It just makes me
HUMAN

Forgive Me

Did I push too hard?
Can I pull back now?
Did I play the emotional card?
I wish I can take it back but how?

If only there was a reverse button
I'd take us back to where we were
When our conversations were not here and there
For your friendship means the world to me

Forgive me please
For all I did
Was out of love & care
This ignorance is just too much to bear

We shall speak again
When you are ready
Like old times
When things weren't this shady

Friendship

Friendship
Is a beautiful thing

Friendship is love
Friendship is kindness
Friendship is selflessness
Friendship is happiness

Friendship is patience
Friendship is caring
Friendship is tolerance
Friendship is understanding

Friendship is bitter
Friendship is painful
Friendship is frustrating
Friendship is a handful

Friendship is forgiving
Friendship is accepting
Friendship is exceptional
Friendship is unconditional

Friendship
It is a beautiful thing

Once Again

Once again
It is me
Making the effort
It is me
Moving us forward

Once again
It is me
Trying to focus
On
Trying to fix us

Once again
I ask myself
'Is this worth it?'

And...

Once again
I find myself
Feeling utterly disappointed
Frustrated
And devastated

The Back-Up Plan

The Back-Up Plan
That is who she is

When there is no one else to talk to
When there is no one else to call
When there is no one else to turn to
When there is no one else at all

The Back-Up Plan
That is who she is

When someone stops all actions
Or when there is no other voice
When they run out of options
And are left with no other choice

Because after all,
She is just That girl
The girl in the Wheelchair
Who will taint the stage
With her 'uncool' appearance
And be nothing
But an interference

Because to everyone
That is who she is

The Back-Up Plan

People Will Never Understand

People will never understand
Your pain

People will never understand
Your sorrow

People will never understand
The true meaning behind your words

People will never understand
The intensity of your racing mind

People will never understand
The indescribable battles you have faced

People will never understand
The utter loneliness of your desolate heart

People will never understand
Your silence

People will never understand
Your genuine intentions

People will never understand
The depths of your despair

People will never understand
The world of agony behind your smile

People will never understand
The wails behind your laughter

People will never understand
The anguish of your soul

People will never understand
No matter how hard you try to construe

People will never understand

But alas,
People do not have to understand
Because Our Lord, The Creator does
And He will answer
Every single prayer
Of His fellow disciples

In Your Eyes

In your eyes
I was always different
Forever a burden
An ungrateful serpent

In your eyes
All that I did
Was never sufficient

The child in me
Longed to play
Yearned to dance
Dreamed to perform

But in your eyes
It didn't look pleasant
A hideous view
A disgraceful presence

Inclusivity
Is all I longed for
Then & Now
Will I ever receive it?
I do not know
But what I do know
Is that in your eyes
I never will

Mind Chatter

The sun has gone down
The sky is filled with clouds
Light taken over by darkness
I'm in the water
Floating
My eyes closing
As I hear birds chirping
And distant mumbling
My mind churning
Frustrated & overwhelmed I'm feeling
Darkness consumeth my being
As I continue sinking
Deeper and deeper
Into the clear blue ocean
I am drowning
But I still fear nothing
For all I long for
Is to be free
Free from the fetters of this world
From all the pain and sorrow
Will there be a tomorrow?
Alas, I do not know

TRAPPED

There was this Bird
Trapped in a locked cage
Alone and Stranded
With no way out
Her cries for an escape
Fell on deaf ears
Her tears intertwined
Together with the raindrops
From the heavy downpour
Night and day felt the same
Her frail & fragile body
Did not match
With her wandering mind
This world was just too suffocating
There was only one thing she felt;
TRAPPED

EMPTY

All my life feels like is
An empty and lonely boat
Each time I try to fill the boat
With love and friendship
A storm arises
And a big wave pushes the boat
And the boat drowns
Together with the empty person inside

Why oh why I ask myself?
Is it self destruction?
Am I the flawed one?
Am I not meant to have any good in my life?
Am I undeserving of love?

For now
There are no answers
Everything is just
EMPTY

ALONE

All my life
Alone I was
No siblings
Only a handful of friends

Nobody to confide in
Nobody to rely on
Cousins were there
But only during long holidays

Imaginary friends
Were my substitute
To the loneliness felt
At home
As a young child

As time went by
Being alone became second nature
And although I did enjoy my alone time
I always longed for companionship
And still do

Someone I could run to
In times of distress
Someone to fill that void
In times of desolation

When Will It Get Better?

Scrolling through my contact list
Names after names I see
But not one person I can reach out to
Not one I can rely on

The pain
The loneliness
The sorrow
When will it get better?

I hate this feeling
This feeling of unworthiness
This feeling of self-loathing
This feeling of resentment

When will it get better?
I do not know

When I'm With You

Light as a feather
Free as a bird
Is how I feel
When I'm with You

The conversations
Flow like a river

The air
Feels fresh again

The wind
Feels chilly
Yet comforting

Smiles from ear to ear
Uncontrollable laughter
In between subtle giggles
Fill the room

A sense of happiness
Never felt before
When I'm with YOU

YOU

You are the Light
In my Darkness

You are the Rainbow
Amidst my Grey Clouds

You are my Sun
And my Moon

Boy do I truly love you
Do you love me too?
Well, I don't think you do
Alas, in silence I shall continue to love you
For in silence, there is no rejection

3 AM

It's 3am
I can't sleep
My mind is racing
So many thoughts churning
Emotions twirling
How did I get here? I ask myself
A simple misunderstanding
Led to a lifetime of blocking
Is this how it is now?
Don't people talk it out anymore?
Has the simple 'block' feature made it easy to delete one another from each other's lives?
Why oh why has it gotten to this?
Why oh why can't I speak my mind?
Why oh why can't I express the truth?
Staying silent is a test
Express my feelings I must
Nonetheless, I'm sorry
But 'Sorry!' doesn't seem to be enough
Perhaps it means nothing to you
But to me it means something
I hope you will eventually see it too

Maybe

Maybe
I am all the things people say I am

Maybe
I am rude
Maybe
I am arrogant
Maybe
I am untrustworthy
Maybe
I am manipulative
Maybe
I am overly sensitive
Maybe
I don't deserve love
Maybe
I don't deserve affection
Maybe
I don't deserve praise
Maybe
I don't deserve happiness

Maybe
This is where I am meant to be

At the edge of a cliff
At the peak of loneliness
At the depths of despair

But Maybe
Just Maybe
I am not all those things people say I am

Maybe
Just Maybe
I am meant to be somewhere else
Somewhere where there is no sorrow
But only joy
Somewhere where there is no darkness
But only light

Maybe
Just...Maybe!

Hurt

When will the tears stop flowing?
When will it all stop hurting?
How will I stop this urge of cutting?
How will I end this miserable feeling?
Oh.. How much I long to feel nothing!

I need to know why
Why did you leave me hanging?
At least tell me something
Anything

It hurts
It hurts too much
'Let it go..' they say
But I can't
I can't let go
Knowing what we had
And what could have been

When will this pain end?
It seems like it never will

Perfectly Imperfect

Long winded
Sensitive
Emotional

Among the names I have been called

Am I those things?
Yes I am!
Am I proud of it?
Yes I am!
Will I change those things about me?
No I won't!
Do I feel those things are a sign of weakness?
No I don't!
Do I have weaknesses?
Of course I do!
Will I change for the better?
God knows I TRY!

Thus,
Judge me NOT
Judge NO ONE
For every single human being
Possesses Imperfections
Imperfections that can also be seen as
Strengths
Indeed a very subjective matter it is
For the One True Judge is
Our Lord, the Creator

I Have A Dream

I Have A Dream!
A dream to see more and more Differently-Abled
individuals being EQUALLY represented in the Mass Media
In Photoshoots
In Billboards
In Magazines
In TV Shows
In Movies
Etcetera, Etcetera

I Have A Dream!
A dream to see EVERYONE
Regardless of
Gender
Race
Ethnicity
Background
Culture
Ability
Size
Shape
or Form
being represented too

I Have A Dream!
To build an Ever Inclusive Society
For our future generation
To be able to live in Peace & Harmony
Whilst embracing each other's differences beautifully

I HAVE A DREAM!

This Is MY DREAM!

A Special Poem By A Doting Mother
To Her Beloved Daughter

Love that is shared
Appears a soul
Why? Oh! Why? You choose me as your mom I wonder?
Care and love
I promised to shower
But HE throws a curve ball
Why? Oh! Why? I wonder?
Pain but pain you endure all your life
No child I wish upon
Your inscrutable countenance gives little away
Radiance, Joy & Expressions of Gratitude holds no limit
Life lessons you learnt at a tender age
'Fear & Answerable to God' you stride to abide

Help is sought by all
And you are there
Be it day or night
In your heart, what you hold
Be it pain or anguish, no one knows
Strong you stay
For God is there by your side
Always

Now you are a woman
And I hope I have done my bit
To please our Father I must
So be as quirky, cheeky and blunt if you must
For I know this for sure
That God has great plans for you
So follow your heart
And He will guide you through
For you are my Precious Gift From God
I LOVE YOU!

Written by

Shaila Sumathi Madhavan

Printed in the United States
By Bookmasters